Writing Timeline

ca. 2500 BCE

Cuneiform tablets produced in Mesopotamia.

1450 BCE

Linear B script developed on the Mediterranean island of Crete.

800 BCE

First examples of what we recognize as the Greek alphabet.

ca. 700 CE

The first quill pens are used in Seville, Spain.

1600 BCE

The Chinese develop a pictorial writing system that is still used today.

ca. 1100 BCE

The Olmec people of central Mexico develop a form of picture writing.

196 BCE

The Rosetta Stone, with its inscriptions in hieroglyphics, demotic Egyptian, and Greek, is carved.

1605

The German-language *Relation*, the first modern newspaper, appears.

863

Cyril and Methodius, Greek brothers, introduce a Greek-based alphabet in Moravia.

1971

Computer programmer Ray Tomlinson sends the first-ever e-mail—to himself.

1439–1450

Johannes Gutenberg develops the first movable-type printing press in Europe.

2011

E-book sales are higher than hardcover sales for the first time in the United States.

783

The first book with lowercase (small) letters is produced for Emperor Charlemagne; it also introduces spaces between words.

1821–1828

Sequoyah produces a written form of the Cherokee language.

Hot Off the Press

Ever since their first appearance more than four centuries ago, newspapers have provided people with the latest information in a fast-changing world. They're a great example of how writing can provide information, education, and even amusement all at the same time.

Although people now get much of this information from other writing sources, such as news sites, blogs, and smartphones, millions of people still like the feel of real paper in their hands each day. At their peak in the late twentieth century, some newspapers printed millions of copies each day. And with their printing presses working hard to cope with those numbers, it's not surprising that a fresh newspaper would be described as being "hot off the press."

Author:

Roger Canavan is an accomplished author who has written, edited, and contributed to more than a dozen books about science and other educational subjects. His three children are his sternest critics—and his fellow explorers in the pursuit of knowledge.

Artist:

Mark Bergin was born in Hastings, England, in 1961. He studied at Eastbourne College of Art and specialises in historical reconstructions, aviation, and maritime subjects. He lives in Bexhill-on-Sea with his wife and children.

Series creator:

David Salariya was born in Dundee, Scotland. He has illustrated a wide range of books and has created and designed many new series for publishers in the UK and overseas. David established The Salariya Book Company in 1989. He lives in Brighton, England, with his wife, illustrator Shirley Willis, and their son, Jonathan.

Editor: **Caroline Coleman**

Editorial Assistant: **Mark Williams**

PAPER FROM
SUSTAINABLE
FORESTS

Published in Great Britain in 2016 by
The Salariya Book Company Ltd
25 Marlborough Place, Brighton BN1 1UB

ISBN-13: 978-0-531-21930-0 (lib. bdg.) 978-0-531-22054-2 (pbk.)

All rights reserved.
Published in 2016 in the United States
by Franklin Watts
An imprint of Scholastic Inc.
Published simultaneously in Canada.

A CIP catalog record for this book is available
from the Library of Congress.

Printed and bound in China.
Printed on paper from sustainable sources.
1 2 3 4 5 6 7 8 9 10 R 25 24 23 22 21 20 19 18 17 16

SCHOLASTIC, FRANKLIN WATTS, and associated logos are trademarks and/or registered trademarks of Scholastic Inc.

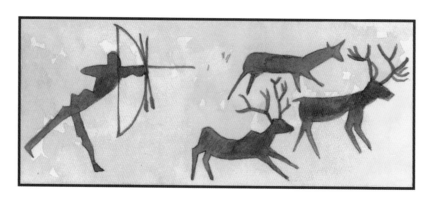

You Wouldn't Want to Live Without™

Writing!

Written by
Roger Canavan

Illustrated by
Mark Bergin

Series created by
David Salariya

Franklin Watts®
An Imprint of Scholastic Inc.

Contents

Introduction

You need to shop for the fifteen guests coming to your birthday party; if writing didn't exist, how would you create a shopping list? How would you know how to work your smartphone? How would you text your friends? How would your birth be recorded? In each of these cases—and dozens more each day—you need to be able to read and write. Just about anything that's important or fun, funny or fascinating, is worth recording.

And that need goes back far into human history— cave dwellers wanted to record the best places to hunt or take shelter. That's where writing comes in. Can you imagine life without it? And what did people do before they could write?

Why Do We Need Writing, Anyway?

We need to communicate with each other to exchange information and to learn. Long ago, human beings learned to speak and then built up advanced languages to express their needs and wishes. Speech—simply talking to one another—was the first communication. But people needed ways to remember what was said, to record what people were talking about a few moments or many years before. Writing was the solution—and we now rely on it all the time.

WRITING can warn and inform us, record the funniest jokes, open our hearts to reveal our innermost feelings, or tell us who won the "big game." It can also help us find what we need to live—when we shop!

DAIRY PRODUCTS

BREAD

MEA

FROM SHOPPING LISTS to product labels to signs, writing provides information that helps us to make decisions.

IMAGINE WHAT LIFE would be like without the pleasure of receiving a handwritten letter, postcard, or Valentine card. Even those few words can mean a lot to the person opening the card.

A simple message can get mixed up without writing it down. Whisper a message to someone, who whispers it to a second person, who whispers it to a third...and ask the tenth to say it out loud. Is it still the same?

ADS IN CITIES surround drivers and pedestrians with written messages. Companies pay lots of money to display those ads, so the messages must get through.

BRAILLE is a system of writing and printing for blind people. Groups of raised dots represent letters of the alphabet. People read Braille by passing their fingertips over the dots.

DANGER

DO NOT FEED ALLIGATOR

BEING ABLE TO READ a message—such as a sign warning of dangers—can mean the difference between life and death. Writing can save lives.

7

Who First Decided to Write?

The roots of what we know as writing go as far back as the cave dwellers, many thousands of years ago. What prompted those early people to begin writing, and how did they go about it? The earliest writing was probably meant to tell others about where to find food or shelter. Some simple marks made with basic tools could get that message across. But humans have always been inventive, and people were soon improving those early forms of writing.

IMAGES on cave walls, lit by flickering flames, told stories of battles, hunting, and how people could protect themselves against animals, the weather, and other people!

Early Forms of Writing

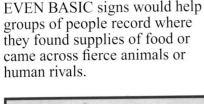

CHINESE scientists (left) have found bones with messages carved by wise men known as oracles. Some of those oracle bones were written more than 3,000 years ago.

You Can Do It!

Flatten your palm on a piece of dampened black construction paper. Sprinkle flour over the paper and your hand. Remove your hand carefully to reveal a cave "painting" of your hand. You're now a cave dweller on the way to inventing real writing!

EVEN BASIC signs would help groups of people record where they found supplies of food or came across fierce animals or human rivals.

PAPER and other materials made writing easier, while people came up with handy inventions such as the quill pen to "put ink to paper."

SOME OF THE EARLIEST writing, called pictographs, used pictures to pass on information. They were a step on the road to alphabets and more advanced writing.

How Do You Get From A to B?

The first real writers lived in societies where people traded what they grew or made. Those people needed to keep track of things. As their methods of farming and transportation advanced, so did the need to record who bought what, how much it cost, and other matters. Rules and laws came into being, and writing had to keep pace. These changes led some people to develop the first alphabets. An alphabet is a set of symbols or letters that represents the sounds of a language, making it easier to record complicated ideas quickly. Later cultures adapted earlier alphabets to fit their changing languages.

								Mouth
								Food
								Man
								Woman

THE SUMERIANS had developed pictographs by 3400 BCE (above). Pictographs used symbols that resembled the objects they described.

THE EPIC OF GILGAMESH, written more than 4,000 years ago, is a stirring tale of Sumerian heroes, written in cuneiform (an ancient Mesopotamian writing system), developed from pictographs.

Many letters used in Russian are based on the same letters in the Greek alphabet. That's because Greek-speaking missionaries introduced writing to the Russians about 1,100 years ago. The columns of letters here show just how alike they still look.

Greek	Russian (Cyrillic)
Αα	Аа
Ββ	Бб
Γγ	Гг
Δδ	Дд
Εε	Ее
Ζξ	Зз
Ηη	Ии

SERIFS—the flared parts at the ends of letters—developed when ancient stone carvers finished with a cross-stroke (right).

HIEROGLYPHICS represented the words and the sounds of the ancient Egyptian language, telling us about the beliefs, history, and daily life of those people.

OLDER ALPHABETS sometimes appear near newer writing. This Italian tomb (above) was marked in Greek 2,000 years ago, when most Italians were using the newer Latin alphabet.

THE MODERN ROMAN ALPHABET shares some letters with the Cyrillic alphabet used in Russian and other East European languages. This sign says "Stop."

11

Hey! What Happened to the Letters?

The author of this book wrote it in English, using the Latin or Roman alphabet, which is a descendant of the Greek alphabet. And the Greek alphabet has links with Phoenician and other writing systems that developed around the Mediterranean. But that region also gave birth to very different kinds of writing, such as the Arabic and Hebrew alphabets. And cultures in other parts of the world built clever systems with a completely different way of linking ideas to images. Some used symbols to represent syllables; others used hundreds—and even thousands—of characters to represent objects and ideas.

THE ANCIENT CHINESE developed an advanced style of writing using thousands of characters. Those characters were often as beautiful as the images in paintings.

Writing Around the World

BRAHMI SCRIPT began in Indian temples about 2,500 years ago. It was one of the first forms of Asian writing to match each sound with an image.

THE MAYAN PEOPLE of Central America developed a writing system more than 2,000 years ago (left). Each symbol represented a word or part of a word.

MOST of the Jewish sacred writings are preserved on scrolls written in Hebrew (right), a language that reads from right to left.

IRISH PEOPLE carved messages honoring the dead on rocks called ogham stones (left). Some are 1,800 years old.

THE ISLAMIC FAITH forbids images of living things, but religious writing in Arabic script can be a work of art in its own right.

Top Tip

When you learn a new language, first find out how it's written. Some languages are written and read from top to bottom, like Chinese; some from left to right, like English; and some from right to left, like Hebrew and Arabic.

Chinese

真書當得其

מנהרות הכותל המערבי
Hebrew

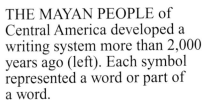

13

Who Knows Their ABCs?

Being able to read and write is a huge advantage in life. Yet for much of human history, most people couldn't. Sometimes, the wealthy and powerful kept this valuable skill to themselves.

But as printing developed—making it easier for people to learn to read—so too did the number of people who could read and write. Most governments nowadays value literacy. They do their best to help schoolchildren get a chance to learn that skill. But even today, there are people who oppose this spread of learning, and some children have to work hard for the right to continue with their schooling.

They went

SCRIBES (professional writers) were among the few ancient Egyptians who could read and write. They spent years practicing, and became very important people.

IRISH MONKS in the Middle Ages added colorful illustrations and even some funny doodles to their religious works. The results were called illuminated manuscripts.

14

Hurry up! I'm one word ahead of you.

To make your own illuminated manuscript, pencil in a word—such as your first name—in large letters, making the first letter really big. Then go over the pencil marks, adding color and patterns along the letters and even in the spaces inside some of the letters.

They went to

IN SOME AREAS of the world, such as West Africa (left), education is not always readily available, so children might not learn to read or write until they are older.

CALLIGRAPHY is the art of fine handwriting (left). Some of the best examples of calligraphy are displayed in museums and art galleries.

WE NEED WRITING and reading skills to use the Internet, but nowadays the Internet is also where many people learn and practice those skills.

Read the passage on the next page and then answer the questions.

15

What Happened to Those Quill Pens?

As more people learned to read and write, they looked for new ways to make the process easier. Along the way, they changed not only the technology of writing, but the way in which we deal with the world as a whole. Quill pens, made from sharpened feathers, made quick writing possible in the Middle Ages. But they were eventually replaced by metal pens, typewriters, and electronic methods of writing. And those changes are continuing faster than ever.

IT IS OFTEN SAID that the modern era of writing began when German goldsmith Johannes Gutenberg developed a printing press (using movable type) around 1450.

"I'm here to save the day!"

¡Estoy aquí para salvar el día!

POPULAR MOVIES have versions with subtitles in dozens of languages so that audiences in other countries can read what's being said. Once again, it's the written word that helps us.

Have an adult help you cut a potato in half. Mark the shape of a letter (in reverse) on each half and cut away the background so that the letter stands out. Press the disk into ink and then onto a piece of paper to print a letter.

Had a gr8 time thx 4 ur present. C u 2mrw :)

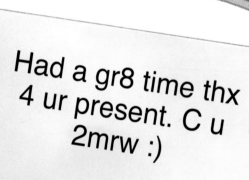

IN THE MID-1800s, the Pony Express (above) went out of business as telegraph cables began to span the United States, offering instant communication. Operators had to translate the coded messages back into ordinary writing.

SOME PEOPLE claim that "text speak" abbreviations (above) and social media word limits harm our writing skills. Others see them as simply new forms of writing.

THE FIRST WORD PROCESSORS, developed in the 1950s, look bulky and clumsy to us, but they paved the way for today's tablets and smartphones.

17

Can You Get By Without Writing?

It is possible to get by somewhat without writing—people had to for thousands of years. Even today, some people find ways of getting a message across without the written word. But could you remember the amount of material that's in a whole book? Or how about using drumbeats to pass on news about you and your family? Wouldn't it be easier to write a quick note or to send a text or e-mail?

IN A WORLD where most people know how to write, those who don't may be at a disadvantage—and stand to lose a lot.

You mean you now own my ranch?

It's right there in the small print.

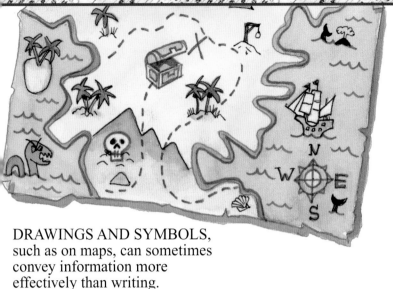

DRAWINGS AND SYMBOLS, such as on maps, can sometimes convey information more effectively than writing.

You Can Do It!

Memory training: Ask a friend to place a group of objects on a table for a minute, then take them away. How many objects can you remember? Try to make a list of them after they are removed.

THE POETS of ancient Greece could recite from memory works lasting many hours. Even today, some people can keep long passages "locked in their heads."

A WEST AFRICAN BOY plays a talking drum, using rhythm or pitch in the drumbeats to spread news to other villages several miles away.

PICTURE GAMES and mime games are a lot of fun, but they also show us how hard it would be to live without writing.

19

Can Writing Mean More Than Words?

riting can go far beyond simply passing on basic information. It can connect people across thousands of miles—and even thousands of years—by expressing feelings that we all share. Whether those words are part of a great work of art, such as a Shakespeare play, or they are contained in a more private message, they touch readers deeply. Distant voices can come alive through writing, and they remain alive in the written word. And some of the simplest writing can mean the most, depending on who's writing it—and who's reading it.

A GET-WELL CARD can mean much more than a wish that someone gets better. It reminds the patient that other people are thinking of her.

THE PLAYS of William Shakespeare, written more than 400 years ago, are still read and performed. Without writing, his work would be unknown now.

ALTHOUGH only several thousand people heard President Abraham Lincoln's Gettysburg Address when he delivered it in 1863, its written version lives on.

ANNE FRANK was a Jewish teenager who wrote a tender diary about her family's life in hiding before being captured by the Nazis during World War II.

SOME PEOPLE will go to great lengths to send messages of love, even if the message is read by thousands of other people on a city street.

Is the Pen Mightier Than the Sword?

The saying that "the pen is mightier than the sword" shows how powerful writing can be. It can improve how people live—but it can also make people's lives harder. Rulers may try to limit what people can read, or try to hide the truth from the public with their own misleading writings. Freedom of speech, one of the most important human rights, makes sure that people are exposed to new ideas. And the way to make that freedom more lasting is to make sure that the speech is preserved as writing.

Protestant reformer Martin Luther uses the written word to spread his ideas (below).

FROM THE MIDDLE AGES, Europeans held religious and political protests in public places. Printing presses helped to spread their ideas.

BRITISH-BORN Thomas Paine wrote *Common Sense* and other protest pamphlets to persuade Americans to declare independence from Great Britain in the 1770s.

COMMON SENSE:

ADDRESSED TO THE

INHABITANTS

OF

A M E R I C A

On the following interesting

S U B J E C T S

I. Of the Origin and Design of Government in general; with concise Remarks on the English constitution.

II. Of Monarchy and Hereditary Succession.

III. Thoughts on the present State of American Affairs.

IV. Of the present Ability of America, with some miscellaneous Reflections.

Written by an ENGLISHMAN

People who feel strongly about a particular subject may start a petition—a letter, signed by many people, asking the government to take action.

MILLIONS of young Chinese in the 1960s carried copies of their leader Mao Zedong's sayings. The "Little Red Book" was one of the most widely published books ever.

HARRIET BEECHER STOWE'S novel about slavery, *Uncle Tom's Cabin*, impressed President Abraham Lincoln. It also stirred up antislavery feelings around the world.

WRITING can urge people to seek peace. Some of the most powerful antiwar feelings were expressed in the poetry of World War I (1914–1918).

23

Can We Always Read What's in Front of Us?

Pictographs, hieroglyphics, and the first alphabets aimed to pass on information clearly to readers. But as newer societies developed, bringing with them new ways of writing, the older systems often became unreadable mysteries. Some writing appears in two or more versions—as on Egypt's famous Rosetta Stone—giving us clues about how to read it. Some people keep their writing secret on purpose, by using codes.

THE TOP SECTION of the Rosetta Stone is written in traditional Egyptian hieroglyphics. It was written by Egyptian priests in 196 BCE to honor King Ptolemy V.

THE MIDDLE SECTION of the stone contains the same message as the top, but written in a simpler form of Egyptian known as demotic.

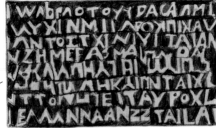

THE LOWEST SECTION of the Rosetta Stone—the same message in Greek—helped scholars to figure out the meaning of the hieroglyphics above.

CARVED SYMBOLS known as Linear B puzzled historians until they recognized them as an early form of the Greek language, written long before the Classical Greek alphabet was developed.

You Can Do It!

Try using one of the simplest secret codes imaginable. A substitution code works by replacing each letter with a different letter or number. Once you've chosen your replacements, make sure to stick with them right to the end.

A = D B = E C = F

NAVAJO SPEAKERS could pass on coded messages in their Native American language during World War II (1939–1945) without the enemy learning it, because few books existed in this language.

ALAN TURING of Great Britain was a brilliant decoder of enemy messages during World War II. His skills led to the development of modern computers.

A QUICK WAY to write in code is to write backward! Unravel the code by reading it in a mirror, which reverses the image.

Can People Write Without Words?

Although literacy is increasing worldwide, it's still important to be able to communicate without words. Why? One obvious reason is that we don't all speak the same language. So an English speaker from the United States might find it hard to read a newspaper in Japan, or a Japanese tourist might struggle to read a menu in Finland. As a result, we come to rely on a number of signs and symbols to take the place of words in some basic messages. And some of those universal messages have even been sent into space, so that maybe even aliens could understand them.

SOME MESSAGES work well without words, especially if they warn people about immediate risks and dangers. Drivers know what to expect on this coast road!

Read the Signs

THE MOST WIDELY USED non-written signs are easy to understand, and are the same whether they're in Sweden or Swaziland. The diagonal line means "don't."

You Can Do It!

Can you think of a way of creating a sign without words, telling people about the time and place of a birthday party? It would have to contain images that anyone could recognize and understand.

T-SHIRTS AND POSTERS often replace words with images, or sometimes mix them together in one message. It's easy to tell which city this girl is visiting.

SOMETIMES you don't have time to stop to read a sign. Two of the most commonly used "signs without words" are those for public toilets.

THE *PIONEER 10* spacecraft's wordless message shows humans, our planet and solar system, and the mission itself—in case creatures from another planet find it.

What's in Store for the Future?

The pace of change keeps getting faster in the modern world. Smartphones, e-books, and tablets help us receive information in an instant. The way in which we gain this information may be superfast and modern, but we're still relying on reading and writing to keep in contact. It's exciting to imagine just how much more connected we all might be in the future, and how easy it will be to read and write the words that will still lie behind that contact. Who knows? Maybe your grandchildren might wind up saying "How did you manage with those clumsy keyboards?" just as we say "How did people get by with quill pens?"

COMPUTERS can study the basic stories that many fairy tales share, and come up with ideas for new ones. But they still need humans to finish the stories.

Maybe I could publish my own book!

NEW TECHNOLOGY makes it possible for people to write and publish their own books without going through a publishing company.

Computers that you wear—as glasses, on your wrist, or as part of your clothing—will bring writing even closer in the future. And you'll be able to update your information instantly, including how far you've run and how fast your heart is beating.

A MODERN LIBRARY (left) is full of ways to read and write, from smartphones and tablets to e-books. Some people even read books printed on paper!

COMPUTERS and music keyboards can help people learn how to write music, and how to match words with that music.

NEED A RECIPE from Australia or the name of a good restaurant in Beijing? Just write to one of your virtual friends to get it.

Glossary

Alphabet A set of symbols in a particular order that represents the sounds of a language.

Braille A system of writing for blind people, using groups of raised dots to represent letters.

Culture The features of everyday life, such as language and education, that a group of people share.

Cuneiform Wedge-shaped symbols that were used as a writing system in ancient Mesopotamia.

Cyrillic An alphabet used in Russia and other Eastern European countries, based on the Greek alphabet.

Demotic Describing the type of simple language used by ordinary people.

Epic A long poem describing the brave actions of an ancient leader or legendary hero.

Goldsmith Someone who makes or sells objects made of gold.

Hieroglyphics A type of writing that uses pictures to represent both words and sounds.

Human right A basic right (such as the right to life and freedom) that any person should have, no matter what type of government is in power.

Illuminated manuscript A religious work that has been copied by hand and decorated with brightly colored pictures.

Mesopotamia A region in southwest Asia between the Tigris and Euphrates rivers (in present-day Iraq).

Middle Ages A period of European history, from 500 to 1500 CE.

Monk A man who joins a religious community, apart from the wider world, to lead a life of prayer.

Movable type A way of printing that uses individual pieces of metal type to create letters and punctuation in a document.

Ogham stone A tall, upright stone found in Ireland and western Britain, engraved with messages in the medieval ogham writing system, which uses notches and lines to represent letters.

Oracle A person who is considered wise and who sometimes makes predictions.

Pamphlet A small book with a paper cover, often containing information or opinions about a single subject.

Petition A request, usually signed by many people, that is presented to people in power.

Pictograph An ancient drawing or painting on a rock.

Printing press A machine that can make many copies of a page—or pages—of text very quickly.

Quill A long wing or tail feather, especially of a goose, that can be shaped into a pen. The sharpened, hollow end is dipped in ink.

Rosetta Stone An ancient stone discovered in Egypt, with the same message carved in ancient Egyptian hieroglyphics, demotic Egyptian, and Greek.

Scribe In a society where few people can read or write, a person who has that skill. In some societies, scribes are very important people.

Subtitles Translations of a foreign film in the audience's language. The translations run along the bottom of the screen.

Talking drum A handheld drum of West Africa, which a drummer can use to tap out messages for other villages, using rhythms that have particular meanings.

Technology Products that are based on the latest scientific advances and are used in a particular field.

Telegraph A system of sending messages over long distances using electrical signals and wires.

Index

The Changing Sound of Language

It's one thing to know how to read old languages, but how do we know what they sounded like? Can we really know what English sounded like in the time of William Shakespeare, about 400 years ago, or in the United States when George Washington was president?

Sometimes we can figure out the sounds of a "dead" language by listening to the languages that developed from it. For example, Italian, Spanish, and French developed from the way people spoke Latin in those countries. Many of the sounds of those modern languages must be similar to the sounds of Latin.

It gets a bit harder with ancient languages that use symbols to represent ideas instead of sounds. But modern languages might also be a good start, if their written rules are similar to those of the older languages. Coptic, Somali, and Arabic—all languages of North Africa—are linked to ancient Egyptian. The language of the pyramid builders probably sounded a lot like those languages.

Checking on how modern languages change is easier. We can look at Shakespeare's plays, for example, to see which words rhymed with each other. The word "prove" rhymed with "love," for example. And descriptions from that time tell us that Shakespeare's Londoners pronounced the *r* in "cart" and "park" rather like most Americans do nowadays. So maybe Romeo and Juliet sounded a little like teenagers from Chicago or Los Angeles!

Top Five Written Words—in Length

English has its share of long words, but it's not the world record-holder in the long-word contest. It's easier to build long words out of lots of smaller words in some other languages, such as German and Turkish. Speakers of those languages sometimes invent long words for the fun of it. How many of these would you get right in a spelling test?

1. Taumatawhakatangihangakoauauotamateaturipukakapikimaungahoronukupokaiwhenuakitanatahu (85 letters)
New Zealand (Maori): the name of a hill, meaning "the summit of the hill, where Tamatea, who is known as the land eater, slid down, climbed up, and swallowed mountains, and played on his nose flute to his loved one."

2. Chargoggagoggmanchaoggagoggchaubunaguhgamaugg (45 letters)
Native American (Nipmuc): the name of a lake in Massachusetts that, according to legend, means "You fish on your side, I'll fish on my side, nobody fishes in the middle."

3. Siebenhundertsiebenundsiebzigtausendsiebenhundertsiebenundsiebzig (65 letters)
German: the word for the number 777,777.

4. Precipitevolissimevolmente (26 letters)
Italian: the longest word in Italian means "as fast as possible."

5. Hippopotomonstrosesquippedaliophobia (36 letters)
English: means "a fear of long words."

Did You Know?

- The word *write* comes from the Old English word *writan*, which means "cut" or "carve." That's because some of the first writing in northern Europe was done by carving the bark of trees.

- A German fishing crew found a sealed old brown bottle in its nets in March 2014. Inside was a note that a young man had written in 1913, making it the oldest "message in a bottle" ever found.

- Many languages put marks over or under letters to change their sound. The Finnish word pääjääjää (meaning "the main stayer") winds up with 14 dots in a row, if you count the two dots over the js.

- A palindrome is a word or phrase that reads the same in reverse. Some examples are "noon," "radar," and "Step on no pets."

- Noah Webster set out to simplify English spellings for Americans in the late 1700s. Many of his changes—such as *honor* and *plow*—took root. But *masheen*, *dawter*, and *tung* are among those that never caught on.

- A typical pencil can draw a line 35 miles (56 kilometers) long or write 45,000 words.

- The American novelist Thomas Wolfe was very tall. It's said that he wrote while standing up, resting the paper on the top of a refrigerator.